Your
Hidden
Gold Mine

$250,000
right under your nose!

Law Steeple, MBA

Author, *Warren Buffett's Investment Secret*

IAN Books

An IAN Books paperback

Published by
IAN Books
41 Watchung Plaza, B242
Montclair, NJ 07042

Cover photo: One kilogram by Swiss Banker

Special sales for educational use by nonprofits.
IANBooksEditor@yahoo.com

ISBN-13: 978-1490340197

ISBN-10: 149034019X

Library of Congress Control Number: 2013942070

For those who need $250,000

IAN Books at <u>Amazon.com</u>

Wealth Without Wall Street:
Buy Direct -- Avoid the Commissions, Fees, Loads

The Insiders' Guides to Buying Discount Financial Services:
Buy Direct and Save $3,000 Every Year

Drop Your Insurance:
Buy Only What You Need

Create Financial Freedom Using Your Wealth Reserve™:
Fix your financial life

The Simple Financial Life:
How to get what you want without going into debt and living
paycheck to paycheck

Build Wealth Without Extra Money or Time:
You don't need to budget or get an extra job

Leah's Money Book:
"I want to control my own money."

The Working Millionaire:
$2,000,000 Tax-FREE Wealth Reserve ™ Self-insure Self-fund

Build Your Own $2,000,000 Tax-FREE Wealth Reserve™:
Self-insure Self-fund your lifestyle

Stop wasting $3,000 every year:
101
financial products *NOT* to buy and why

Wealth:
What every high school graduate needs to know in the 21st century

Contents

Introduction

What happened to your tax refund this year?
It could be your $250,000 **Gold Mine**.
Use a special IRS-approved account for tax-FREE income.
Spend all of the $250,000—NO taxes EVER.

The average tax refund was $3,022. If you had invested your refunds since you started loaning part of your paycheck to our Congress, you might have $250,000 by now.

What did you do with your refund this year? Most of us can't remember. Just think if you had started investing it earlier. Study the table below. This is your *Gold Mine*. Investing $3,000—$250 a month, $9 a day—can turn into $250,000 or more.

Compounding is how it happens—money earning money on its earnings every period. Invest your money in businesses sharing profits with you and over time you can reach $1,000,000.

When we invest in successful businesses, we can earn 10% to 12% a year. After 10 years, we can have $55,000 because the businesses paid dividends and we reinvested them. After 25 years, we could have $250,000 and after 33 years, perhaps $1,000,000. Over time, stocks are safer than bank CDs because we earn more than inflation subtracts. We have buying power.

Compounding works best when we put our money to work in successful businesses paying us dividends and stock splits. When we use a low-cost tax-FREE account, we avoid fees AND taxes so we **keep more** of our money to compound. The table below gives us some idea of how fast our investment can grow if we invest it in businesses like the ones we use every day.

Monthly Accumulation at 12% per year									
	5	10	15	20	25	30	35	40	45	50
$100	$8,167	$23,004	$49,958	$98,925	$187,884	$349,496	$643,095	$1,176,477	$2,145,469	$3,905,834
$200	$16,334	$46,008	$99,916	$197,850	$375,768	$698,992	$1,286,190	$2,352,954	$4,290,938	$7,811,668
$300	$24,501	$69,012	$149,874	$296,775	$563,652	$1,048,488	$1,929,285	$3,529,431	$6,436,408	$11,717,502
$500	$40,835	$115,020	$249,790	$494,625	$939,420	$1,747,480	$3,215,475	$5,882,385	$10,727,346	$19,529,169

This kind of investment return is **possible but not guaranteed**. But wouldn't you rather have $1 million, more or less, than $150,000 in the bank? According to Buffett, investing is all about "laying out money now to get more money back in the future ... after inflation." It is a risk . . . but a risk the wealthy are taking using simple investing steps.

Are you willing to trade your $3,000 annual tax refunds for $250,000 in the future? This is what the smartest investor does.

> ## "My wealth has come from a combination of living in America, some lucky genes, and <u>compound interest</u>." *Warren Buffett*

People with a lot of money already know that the **miracle of compounding** is what keeps their wealth growing. Like them, we can invest in a number of successful businesses. Even if one fails, we can still earn 10-12% a year over time. We can still mine gold.

Compounding works best if we do *NOT* have to pay tax on the earnings and broker/advisor fees every year. That way ALL of our earnings are reinvested for the next period. This illustrates what happens to tax-FREE compounding over time.

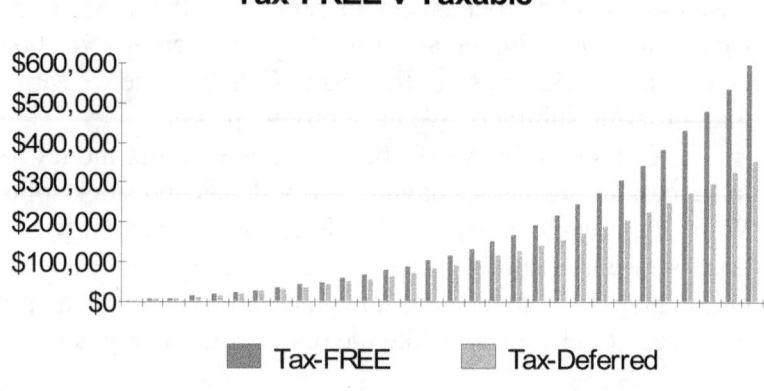

Tax-FREE v Taxable

If you don't receive a tax refund of $3,000 or you want to stop loaning the Congress your money, you can invest a fixed amount like $250 or $500 a month (about $9 a day for each of you). If we set up the account to invest automatically, we won't forget to send a check every month. Compounding works with regular mining.

I will show how to set up your <u>Gold Mine</u> in only one hour. Fortunately, low-cost mutual funds and tax-FREE trusts are now readily available. You can easily avoid Wall Street's fees of 1-3% and all taxes FOREVER. We follow simple steps and we benefit from the FULL **miracle of compounding**. Many people like you have become wealthy over time this way. And now the steps have been made easy to execute. You can do it yourself in an hour.

For most people, a $250,000 **Gold Mine** right under their nose is invisible. Why? This **Gold Mine** is not a lottery. We have to dig for each chunk—one deposit at a time—but automatically. We bring out $8,000 for each $3,000 we put in. If we keep mining, we can bring out $30,000 for each $3,000. We **turn our wasted tax refund into a $1 million Gold Mine**.

The wealthy are mining their **Gold Mine** every day. If you are paying off a car loan or other debt, you are working in their Gold Mine for them. They got there by living below their means so they could invest. They invest in their own business or the businesses owned by the mutual funds they buy every month. My successful clients let their money work for them!

With a special IRS-approved tax-FREE account, we have an investment edge over the very wealthy. I will show how to use this IRS tax haven so it will provide you with a tax-advantaged income source all your life. If we use this account correctly, the tax-FREE status is worth over $75,000 extra to us. Taxes are the greatest killer of wealth. The key factor in building wealth is **maximizing the miracle of compounding**. We need to grow our wealth in a tax-FREE account AND pay low fees.

This tax-FREE account, called a "**Wealth Reserve**ᴹ" by my colleague, Dan Keppel, grows without taxation as it accumulates. Unlike a regular account, we don't pay taxes every year on the dividends or value our account earns. When we let our balance compound, we can reach $250,000 in about 20 years, $1 million in 33. We can do this because we invest in a proven long-term investment—as part of growing companies worldwide.

2nd Benefit: After we accumulate a sizable balance—say $75,000—we can borrow from it to buy things like appliances and luxury cars. We pay cash and avoid paying interest to others' Gold Mines. We can also use it to cover our insurance deductibles and save paying some premium amounts. Of course larger risks are covered by our regular high-deductible policies.

The **miracle of compounding** works best if we use a mutual fund account at the lowest cost we can find. I show how to set up a low-cost "**Wealth Reserve**™" at no cost. I will show you how to pick low-cost investments for long-term growth. We don't need to pay a broker or sales person to decide which securities to buy. In fact, the average investor can lose 40% of their total to Wall Street.

Another benefit of this trust account is that it allows us to make equal contributions monthly. When we stop loaning Congress our money, we reduce the taxes taken from us each paycheck. This provides us with the mining "expenses" of $250 a month.

This is called "dollar cost averaging." It is convenient to invest the same amount monthly. If you and your spouse contribute $250 a month, each of you could have $1,000,000 or your family could reach $1 million in about 25 years. By investing a fixed amount each month, we can buy shares at the least cost possible. We buy more shares when the price is low and fewer when high.

If our investing is done automatically, we have a better chance of success. **Automatic mining** makes it certain. Consistency is important in mining our **Gold Mine**. We can't keep mining without paying the "expenses." The money comes out of our bank account so we reach $250,000 in the future. This is why the wealthy get richer every hour, day, year. They never stop mining.

The **Wealth Reserve**™ may be the best way to accumulate for retirement if your employer does NOT match your deposits or offer low-cost investment options. However, you can contribute much more to a 401k than a **Wealth Reserve**™ –up to $17,500 (2013) versus $5,500. Both accounts will compound earnings. One will be **tax-FREE** now AND in retirement. The point of both accounts is for contributions to grow without taxes for a number of years. It is best to start with a **Wealth Reserve**™ which has a limit of $5,500. It may provide higher long-term accumulations than a 401k because there are zero, $0 taxes, ever.

Unlike other methods of investing for the future, a **Wealth Reserve**™ can provide a lifetime of tax-FREE growth. This is a powerful strategy! It uses the most powerful financial force available—**compounding** of high earnings over time. It avoids the greatest **killer** of wealth-building—TAXES. We pay no taxes on the accumulations and no taxes on the withdrawals later. And we don't pay broker or advisor fees every year either.

Below are 10 steps to mining your **Gold Mine**. We invest in high-earning securities over a period of time. We let compounding turn our $3,000 "shovels" into $30,000 bars. We spend $99,000 for a $1,000,000 over time. We don't stop mining when the market goes up or down. We mine every month like the wealthy do. That is how we gain $250,000 to $1 million from our **Gold Mine**.

I will explain the steps to mine your first $250,000:

1. Create a tax-FREE account.
2. Use a tax-favored account for lifetime savings.
3. **Compound** high earnings over time.
4. Automate monthly contributions to ensure success.
5. Use low-cost mutual funds only.
6. Buy groups of stocks of growing companies worldwide.
7. Spend less than you earn.
8. Buy only the products you need—save $3,000 a year.
9. Manage the account only once a year.
10. Spend $250,000 tax-FREE income.

Building wealth requires patience. If you are self-employed, you understand that it takes time to build a business. You have to have the right product and then find the customers to serve at a price that enables you to earn a living and profit to expand.

If you work for others, you don't have to be a genius to become financially independent. Wealthy people control their spending by various methods. Some have goals and budgets that help them build their spending and investing habits. Some are thrifty and don't spend more than they make. Some don't try and just have the trustee debit their checking account every month.

Wealthy people have learned that there is no quick way to become wealthy. Accumulating assets requires the investing habit. They learned the habit and saw that the habit paid off over time. They let the miracle of compounding work. They pay fewer taxes and fees. Almost all their money compounds making more gold.

It does not take a lot of time to manage your account. In fact, it takes only an hour to set up a **Wealth Reserve**™ and takes only 1 hour per year to manage it.

As master investor Warren Buffett said:

Building wealth is more about *NOT* doing something with your investments. Activity in investing usually is the result of fear or greed. Activity usually costs more than the gains. Don't tamper with the mining gear, in other words.

People with assets cultivate **patience**. They don't panic when their account goes down. In fact, they buy more assets when others are selling. They know they cannot build a small fortune overnight with a quick buy and sell strategy. Patience allows your hidden gold mine to grow by itself. Wealthy people buy assets that grow—earnings on earnings, interest on interest. Note on page 22 that the client's account keeps growing even after falling some years. The client never lost money because they did NOT sell in lean years! Consistent mining finds the gold.

People with assets understand that to build wealth they need to keep their money working. They do this by buying only the products they need. In fact, that has become their way of life. For instance, they can afford to buy an expensive new car but they don't. They know that new cars lose value. foxbusiness.com/personal-finance/2013/04/03/depreciation-5-car-models-that-lose-value-fast/ The money they save adds to their wealth so they can reach their goals quicker. They invest in the businesses they own or in the securities of successful companies. They improve their future by buying more assets that "grow by themselves." The chart on page 32 illustrates annual growth since 1950.

Wealthy people know about the **miracle of compounding**. Isn't it time we all learn. If we invest $250 per spouse, we may have $1 million in 25 years. $250 a month is only $9 a day. That $9 a day is building our future life.

Turn $9 a day into $1,000,000

Monthly	Accumulation at 12% per year									
	5	10	15	20	25	30	35	40	45	50
$100	$8,167	$23,004	$49,958	$98,925	$187,884	$349,496	$643,095	$1,176,477	$2,145,469	$3,905,834
$200	$16,334	$46,008	$99,916	$197,850	$375,768	$698,992	$1,286,190	$2,352,954	$4,290,938	$7,811,668
$300	$24,501	$69,012	$149,874	$296,775	$563,652	$1,048,488	$1,929,285	$3,529,431	$6,436,408	$11,717,502
$500	$40,835	$115,020	$249,790	$494,625	$939,420	$1,747,480	$3,215,475	$5,882,385	$10,727,346	$19,529,169

1

Create a tax-FREE account

Mining our $1 million tax-FREE **Gold Mine** takes time. It is a business and takes patience. It is easier than starting our own store. We would have to find and sell the right products to the right customers in a profitable manner. It is difficult to come up with a completely new way compete with others.

We can strike gold right under our nose! All we need to do is take some of our salary from working for others and invest it. We can accumulate $250,000 then $1,000,000 over time. Using the stocks of growing companies, it takes about 25, then 33 years.

Our Gold Mine is a special IRS-approved account that gives us an advantage over wealthy people so we can become wealth too. This account allows us to take out our gold without federal or state income taxes after we have worked our mine for a while. This can give us an extra 30% or so to spend. It also helps us grow our account to $1 million faster.

If we are going to accumulate $1,000,000 in about 33 years, we need to find investments that can earn 10% to 12% a year, year after year. If we want to have a balance of $1 million, we would have to wait 100 years for our $250 a month to grow in a bank at 3%. Banks pay low interest because they guarantee to pay interest every day or every month all the time. The bank is a safe place to put your money if you need it within a year. It is not good for long-term investing.

Investing in stocks provides almost the reverse risk profile. Historically, the value of a stock market index—a bunch of stocks —has varied greatly in any one year. However, over time, the value has ALWAYS increased. This is the reason wealthy people have most of their money in the stocks of growing companies.

Remember, we are looking for an investment that compounds our money at 10-12% a year. The reward and risk profile of owning a bunch of stocks is like owning a business—in any one year, we might have a loss or we might profit. But over time we have more profits than losses and thus succeed.

Range of annual returns of stocks, 1950 – 2000

Bank savings are a great place to park our money for a year in case we need it to repair our car, appliances or house. However, bank savings are not really an investment. People who put all their money in the bank because they think it is "safe" are not thinking about the long-term. They are actually losing money. Inflation is eating away at the value of their savings.

Inflation is historically about 3%. If we earn 3% or less on our money, we are losing purchasing power. This means that it costs $0.46 to mail a first class letter instead of 6 cents as it did in 1970. Sending a letter went up at about 5% a year. In order to have enough money to mail a letter in retirement, we are going to need to invest our LONG-TERM money in an investment earning more than 5%. This goes for all the money we will need to buy everything we will need in the future.

There are few investments that we can buy that have the same long-term annual returns of stocks of growing companies. The graph below presents the relative growth of different types of investments and inflation. Over long-periods of time, government bonds grow at a rate a little above the rate of inflation. Large company stocks like GE and P&G grow at a higher rate and thus accumulate larger values in our account. Smaller companies grow much faster and make our account even larger over time. However, as the graph shows, the index line can be very jagged on a monthly and even yearly basis. Values do go up over time.

Index Line Graph: Frequency: Monthly

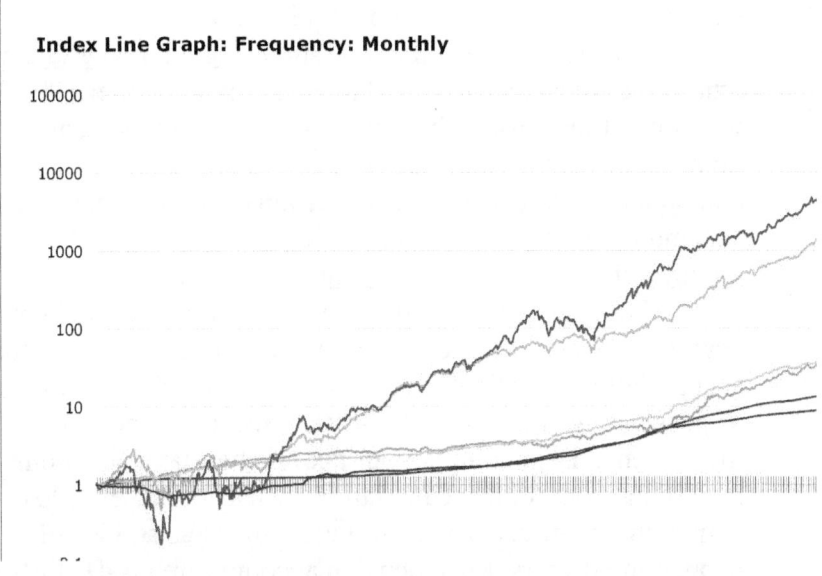

Top line—Small Cap Stocks
2nd line—Large Cap Stocks (S&P 500)
3rd line—US Long-term Corporate Bonds
4th line—Intermediate-term Government Bonds
5th line—US 30 day Government T-bills
6th line—US inflation

Courtesy: Dr. Campbell R. Harvey http://www.duke.edu/~charvey/

This graph makes it pretty clear that in order to accumulate $1,000,000 from monthly contributions, we must buy and hold the securities of growing companies worldwide AND pay **zero** tax on the growth to maximize compounding. We can see clearly that investing in growing company stocks is more likely to get us to our goal in our lifetime than investing in government bonds or a bank savings account.

This graph shows the accumulation over time without paying taxes each year on our earnings or annual fees to an advisor or broker. It does show that over most periods greater than 10 years, our account value grows more with stocks.

Some wealthy people also invest in gold, real estate, and alternative investment schemes. But these investments do NOT usually represent a large portion of their portfolio. These investments do not come without significant costs and significant risk. They do NOT show the same consistent long-term growth pattern that global growing companies show.

According to a number of studies, gold, real estate and other investments have annual average returns under 10%. When we subtract the costs of buying, maintaining and securing these investments, we give up a lot of the gains. We can use an online compounding calculator to become familiar with total accumulations at different rates of return—3, 5, 7, 9, 11, etc. moneychimp.com/calculator/compound_interest_calculator.htm

For instance, if an investment requires taxes to be paid each year, this cancels some of the compounding effect on the total accumulation over time. Since we wish to reach $1 million as soon as possible, we must use a tax-FREE account to hold our investments. Depending on our tax bracket (taxable income) we may reduce our total accumulation by half because we lose the compounding effect. The chart below gives us an idea of what can happen in 30 years. Most pension accounts are tax-DEFERRED not tax-FREE. Taxes have to be paid sometime.

As you have probably guessed, the wealthy have already figured out how to pay less tax on their wealth. The American tax system taxes earned income at higher rates than investment income. Thus we must pay federal and state income taxes, excise taxes, Social Security and Medicare taxes, perhaps unemployment and disability income taxes as well as sales tax on most goods.

For the wealthy, like Warren Buffett, with $53 billions of assets, most of his income is from his company stock gains and dividends. He admitted, "I pay at a lower overall tax rate than all of my office employees." He pays only 17% **total** tax. Listen and weep: http://www.youtube.com/watch?v=Cu5B-2LoC4s.

We are not at that stage yet. Most of us have income which is taxed as earned income and goes straight to the government before we have a chance to pay less tax. Even self-employed people must pay taxes as they go—at least once a quarter.

In order for us to become wealthy we must find a way to avoid paying tax on our $1,000,000 account as it accumulates. Traditional pensions, 401k and IRAs just delay taxes—taxes must be paid later as the money comes out of the account AND at higher earned income tax rates. Thus even when our investment money is growing it is converted to earned income money for tax purposes. Unlike Mr Buffett, we NEVER get to pay the wealthy people rate of 15%.

Tax-FREE v Taxable

Luckily, there is now a solution for us to match the tax advantage that the wealthy. In fact, only we can use it.

Summary: Create a tax-FREE account.

We use a tax-FREE trust to compound the high returns of the stocks of growing companies over time. We avoid the greatest killer of wealth—taxes—and let time transform our $99,000 in contributions into $1 million. Patience and steady investing make our strategy beat the industry myth of genius stock pickers. We become millionaires by using the *miracle of compounding.*

Monthly	Accumulation at 12% per year									
	5	10	15	20	25	30	35	40	45	50
$100	$8,167	$23,004	$49,958	$98,925	$187,884	$349,496	$643,095	$1,176,477	$2,145,469	$3,905,834
$200	$16,334	$46,008	$99,916	$197,850	$375,768	$698,992	$1,286,190	$2,352,954	$4,290,938	$7,811,668
$300	$24,501	$69,012	$149,874	$296,775	$563,652	$1,048,488	$1,929,285	$3,529,431	$6,436,408	$11,717,502
$500	$40,835	$115,020	$249,790	$494,625	$939,420	$1,747,480	$3,215,475	$5,882,385	$10,727,346	$19,529,169

Various investment accumulations

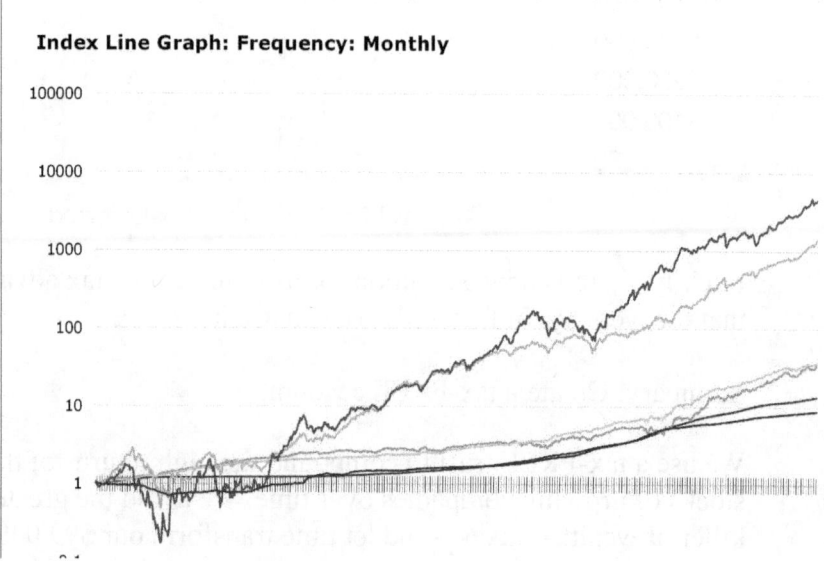

Index Line Graph: Frequency: Monthly

Top line—Small Cap Stocks
2nd line—Large Cap Stocks (S&P 500)
3rd line—US Long-term Corporate Bonds
4th line—Intermediate-term Government Bonds
5th line—US 30 day Government T-bills
6th line—US inflation

Courtesy: Dr. Campbell R. Harvey http://www.duke.edu/~charvey/

2

Use a tax-favored account for lifetime savings

The solution to our problem came in 1997. Senator Roth introduced the Roth IRA. This tax-FREE account we call a **Wealth Reserve**™ provides the protection we need to allow our contributions to compound without taxation every year AND later when we take them out, we never have to pay taxes on the earnings, dividends and interest we earn on our money. We don't even pay the tax-advantaged rate of the wealthy!

Ben Franklin was wrong! Only death is certain, not taxes. The only thing we give up with this account is an immediate tax deduction. However, compare the value of paying a little more tax, $450 (15%-25% on $3,000) now, with paying ZERO tax later. We can spend $30,000 tax-FREE for every $3,000 a year we contributed over time. We can see the fantastic advantage we now have. This is a better deal than most wealthy people have.

Tax-FREE accumulation and tax-FREE income after age 59.5 is a huge bonus. It is like receiving $300,000 FREE on our $1 million account. Also, because we already paid tax on the contributions, we pay no tax when we take the money out during our lifetimes. This can make a big impact on our borrowing costs when we take money out to buy an appliance, a car, or a down payment. We can also save insurance premiums too.

Using this account, our total contributions of $99,000 over time grow to over $1,000,000 and we don't have to pay any federal or state income tax on the earnings. WOW! Since we pay no tax, Uncle Sam is really helping us out in meeting our goal. All we have to do is use this special IRS tax haven and keep making contributions. We set it and forget it.

This special account is the IRS §408 Roth IRA trust we call our "**Wealth Reserve**™". We have to follow the rules to gain this amazing tax advantage but the Roth IRA rules are pretty simple— taxed money goes in and tax-FREE earnings come out after age 59 ½. We can take our contributions out anytime.

Why is this account special? Every other type of investment account requires that taxes be paid now or later. Mutual funds declare gains each year just like a bank CD and we need to pay tax. Our retirement accounts and annuities are tax-deferred. We pay tax when we take money out. Even life insurance with cash value requires taxes to be paid unless it is a death benefit to heirs. Even assets like individual stocks or ETFs or our own company equity held for long term gains will require taxes eventually when sold. The gains in a **Wealth Reserve**™ are FREE—no tax ever.

Contributions are limited to $5,500 (2013), but may rise in future years. http://www.irs.gov/publications/p590/ch02.html There are income limits but most people don't hit the earnings limit of $127,000 (2013) until later. If we are married, the limit is $188,000 (2013). We make our deposit to our **Wealth Reserve**™ automatic so we can't forget to do it each month.

We may also invest in our employer's Roth 401k if it is offered. The contributions grow tax FREE forever. We can contribute up to $17,500 (2013). We will have tax-FREE income from the account later.

We can make contributions to our Roth 401k only if our employer offers it in the retirement plan. Many young people prefer to be taxed at the beginning of their careers since their salaries do not draw high tax rates yet. The contribution limit may be raised in the future.

There are no limits on an employee's income in determining if he or she can make designated Roth 401(k) contributions. If we decide to invest $10,000 a year for 22 years in a low-cost stock fund inside our employer's Roth 401k plan, we could accumulate $1 million with NO income taxation to pay on the earnings. The tax savings might be worth an extra 30% since our federal and state tax payments are avoided.

The catch: If we take the *earnings* out before age 59.5, we must pay income tax, unless we use $10,000 for our first home, are disabled, or die. The account must be open at least 5 years to take money out. However, if we take out *contributions*, we pay no tax. If we pay our 'loan' back to our own account, we can still reach our goal. The hard part is leaving our money alone to grow tax-FREE.

Let's say we need $10,000 to buy a new used car. As we can see from the chart on page 22, taking $10,000 from an account worth $50,000 is very different from taking $10,000 from one worth only $25,000. Both are contributions and are not taxable but borrowing 40% of the account this early stunts its growth.

Our working millionaire would find a way to save the $10,000 separately or keep driving the old car. The power of compounding is too valuable to lose by raiding the account too early. One story about billionaire Buffett will illustrate the habits of the wealthy. Mr Buffett is said to have driven (no chauffeur) his VW Beetle long after he became a multibillionaire. Buffett did not like to lose money and a new car loses 40% of its value quickly. He thought that the $25,000 a new car cost, invested at 12%, is worth about $80,000 in 10 years. So he kept driving the old VW.

Monthly Accumulation at 12% per year									
	5	10	15	20	25	30	35	40	45	50
$100	$8,167	$23,004	$49,958	$98,925	$187,884	$349,496	$643,095	$1,176,477	$2,145,469	$3,905,834
$200	$16,334	$46,008	$99,916	$197,850	$375,768	$698,992	$1,286,190	$2,352,954	$4,290,938	$7,811,668
$300	$24,501	$69,012	$149,874	$296,775	$563,652	$1,048,488	$1,929,285	$3,529,431	$6,436,408	$11,717,502
$500	$40,835	$115,020	$249,790	$494,625	$939,420	$1,747,480	$3,215,475	$5,882,385	$10,727,346	$19,529,169

Most clients are not that thrifty. They use their contributions to buy a used car to avoid new car depreciation and new appliances, vacations, and other necessities AFTER they have a sizable account. When both family wage earners contribute to their Roth IRAs, they can easily reach a quarter of a million dollars in 15 years. That means $90,000 are contributions and then some of it can be used to pay cash instead of buying on credit.

Wealthy people use their wealth to pay cash because then they never PAY interest. Paying interest on a debt is the reverse of compounding. Someone else is becoming wealthy from us. The wealthy always EARN interest. See the video for the real cost: Khanacademy.org/science/core-finance/interest-tutorial/cont-comp-int-and-e/v/introduction-to-compound-interest-and-e. The real cost of buying something on credit is shocking. Buffett thinks, Why give up $80,000 when I can drive the old car a little longer. Buffett could have bought 100 new cars and it wouldn't have changed his wealth or lifestyle, but he didn't. His habit is to live frugally and not look wealthy.

We can use this account (its contributions) to cover our liability **insurance deductibles** also. We can save thousands of dollars by using the highest deductibles on our car, home and health insurance. **Self-insurance** is also the way to avoid any changes in our policy costs. Insurers are less likely to drop us if we don't make claims for small amounts. If we take care of our out-of-pocket medical expenses, we may find a low-cost comprehensive policy if we need to buy health coverage.

The rules for the use of our "**Wealth Reserve**™" account are manageable by ourselves. We don't need an advisor. They are found at irs.gov/retirement/article/0,,id=137307,00.html. Our account trustee can answer most questions. We don't need to pay an attorney. All of the large low-cost mutual funds firms are IRA trustees. We will discuss the best firms available below.

We can start this account with any of the firms with no upfront charges. Most do charge an annual fee for the investments and an annual bookkeeping fee. We will consider the specific investment options later. We will use only low-cost firms.

It is important to pick a trustee with the least costs since over time the annual costs can really destroy our accumulations. For instance, if we use a brokerage firm as trustee, we might have to pay 2% or more each year on the balance. The difference is huge. If both spouses have a low-cost account with contributions of $250 a month for 33 years, they could accumulate $2,000,000. If they use a high-cost broker/advisor, both accounts may hit only $900,000. Depending on earnings of 8-10% using a broker/advisor (fees of 2% per year), they could really hurt themselves. We need to watch the costs. We will compare firms below.

We can open our account at any age as long as we have *earned* income. Stock dividends or interest do not count. Any job will do. We don't even need a job requiring a W-2 to prove it. A part-time, weekend or night job will do. Any cash-only work will also qualify. Accountants recommend that receipts and records be maintained. We could even work for ourselves in a home-office business.

Nontaxable distributions from a Roth IRA won't affect our eligibility for student aid either. Later, in retirement, this money won't affect our social security benefits as of the rules today.

We can make contributions to both our individual Roth IRA and our Roth account at work (401k, 403b, 457b). The limits change each year, so check Pub 590: http://www.irs.gov/pub/irs-pdf/p590.pdf. The 2013 limits are $5,500 ($1,000) and $17,500 ($5,500) respectively. (If we are age 50 or older, we can make a catch-up contribution to both.)

Summary: Use a tax-favored account to self-insure.

Avoiding taxes on our annual gains supercharges our accumulations. This special account is the IRS §408 trust we call a **"Wealth Reserve™"**. We have to follow the rules of a Roth IRA to gain this amazing tax advantage. The rules are pretty simple: pay smaller tax on contributions now in exchange for NO tax on huge gains later. We can use the contributions to avoid paying interest to banks for our major purchases. We earn interest, we don't pay interest. We use the account to self-insure some insurance liabilities. The **Wealth Reserve™** is the perfect tax shelter for working people. And it is free to set up and run each year. In the future, we can spend tax-FREE $30,000 for every $3,000 we invest today. That is the *Miracle of Compounding.*

Actual client Tom's account, investing $3,000 per year, 1962-2003

24%	3,720
16%	7,795
12%	12,091
-10%	13,582
24%	20,561
11%	26,153
-8%	26,821
4%	31,013
14%	38,775
19%	49,713
-14%	45,333
-26%	35,766
37%	53,110
24%	69,576
-8%	66,770
6%	73,956
18%	90,809
32%	123,827
-5%	120,486
22%	150,653
21%	185,920
6%	200,255
32%	268,297
19%	322,843
5%	342,135
17%	403,808
32%	536,987
-3%	523,787
31%	690,091
8%	748,538
10%	826,692
2%	846,286
38%	1,172,015
23%	1,445,268
33%	1,926,197
28%	2,469,372
21%	2,991,570
-9%	2,725,059
-12%	2,403,420
-22%	1,874,601
29%	2,412,905

3

Compound high earnings over time

Compounding high earnings is key. The rich get richer—the top
1% take 23.5% of all income (up from 8.9%). And, as many
millionaires have said, "the first million is the hardest." If we start
with $3,000, it will take us 33 years of investing $3,000 a year in
stock funds to reach $1,000,000. (And only in a tax-FREE
account.) However, when we reach a million dollars, we only have
to double our money to reach $2 million. Investors in stock funds,
earning 10-12% on average, do this in 7-9 years without adding
new money. Our tax-FREE low-cost account makes it easier to
reach our goal.

Compounding of high earnings means that we make money on
our last period's accumulations. The progression looks like the
client's account values on the previous page. Notice that our
balance can double in a couple of good years. This happens
because we are not just adding $3,000 per year, but adding up to
38% of the previous year's accumulation to our balance. We are
making money on top of our money with no extra effort on our
part. During this 40 year period, this client lost money some years.
In fact, they lost 14% and then 26% back to back, but then made
37% and 24%.

Wealthy people don't panic. They have learned that
compounding over the long-term is the only way they can build
wealth. There are no successful get rich quick schemes. To reach
their goal, they know there will be setbacks. No business grows
steadily upward all the time. They have seen the losses before and
they don't sell their assets in a panic.

We will buy assets that "grow by themselves." We will have
security because our _**purchasing power**_ will grow over time. If we
doubt that the wealthy invest in the stock market for security, take
a look at the long-term returns for various Vanguard mutual funds
where they put their money. These funds have provided investors

with $1,000,000 or more for their retirement. During the recent recessions, Vanguard had investor inflows not outflows.

The wealthy earn 10% to 12% on their money. We could buy all ten Vanguard funds and receive 11.5% total return with less risk than owning just one fund. When one fund is down, others are up.

2012 Total Return	Fund	Long-term Return	Longevity
15.8%	500 Index	10.5%*	since 1976
2.7%	Energy	12.3%	since 1984
18.3%	Extended Market	10.3%	since 1987
15.1%	Health	16.3%	since 1984
20.0%	International Growth	10.8%	since 1981
15.3%	PRIMECAP	12.9%	since 1984
18.0%	Small Cap Index	10.4%	since 1960
10.1%	Wellesley Income	10.2%	since 1970
20.8%	Windsor	11.2%	since 1958
16.7%	Windsor II	10.4%	since 1985
15.3%	Average	11.5%	

*Average Annual Returns as of 12/31/12.

This kind of security comes from our regular contributions … and patience. The miracle of compounding works its magic on our **Wealth Reserve**™ when we give it TIME. The wealthy give their money time to work. They don't take it out. They avoid paying tax on the gains. They maintain their contribution schedule because each $100 added is worth $10,000 to them later. They use the compound interest calculator so they know the future value: moneychimp.com/calculator/compound_interest_calculator.htm.

Compounding of high earnings requires patience but has a big bang. Most people who become wealthy have learned that slow growth is the only real growth. At the beginning of the accumulation, especially if we have a loss or two, we are very tempted to get discouraged and quit making contributions. The account just doesn't seem to adding up to an inspiring total.

It took my client 21 years to get to $150,000. Then it only took 14 years to get to a $1,172,015. After only 4 years, it became $3,000,000. Shortly thereafter he "lost" over a million dollars!

This client stuck with it and was successful in reaching the goal but there are many who did not. Most people who are not wealthy already, have a hard time believing it can happen with their patience. They just don't have the experience of how compounding works to keep faith in its outcome eventually.

If you already have a **Wealth Reserve**™ with significant values, you can use it to do your gift and estate planning. You don't have to take the money out beginning at age 70½, as with a regular IRA or pension. You can let it grow. You can name your family members as beneficiaries which will be effective for both property law and income tax purposes. Obviously, as beneficiary, your grandchild could just liquidate the account and thus lose the value for their "Gift of a Lifetime." Wealthy people use a knowledgable attorney to make sure their wealth passes to those who make the most of it.

Once an account becomes sizable, we don't need to add contributions to it. Usually, by the time we stop regular employment, we aren't making contributions. This account cannot accept contributions unless they are the result of *earned* income. Some wealthy people continue to work after age 65 because they love what they do and want to continue. Obviously, they don't need to work. Compounding continues nevertheless.

One of the best examples of the potential of growth by compounding is seen in the accumulation of investor Anne Scheiber. With below average wages, this woman invested in quality companies which paid dividends and gains. She reinvested her dividends and gains and at her death gave $22 million to her favorite charity. Consistency wins.

Hear how Earl Crawley did it: http://www.youtube.com/watch?v=XD0svDGyLWU

Summary: Compound high earnings over time.

Getting "the first million is the hardest." Since we don't make millions, compounding high earnings is the only way we are going to reach our goal in our lifetime. Compounding works because we leverage TIME in our favor.
That is what Warren Buffett means by saying,

"...our favorite holding period is **forever.**"
http://www.berkshirehathaway.com/letters/1988.html

The annual returns of growing companies

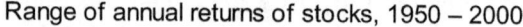

Range of annual returns of stocks, 1950 – 2000

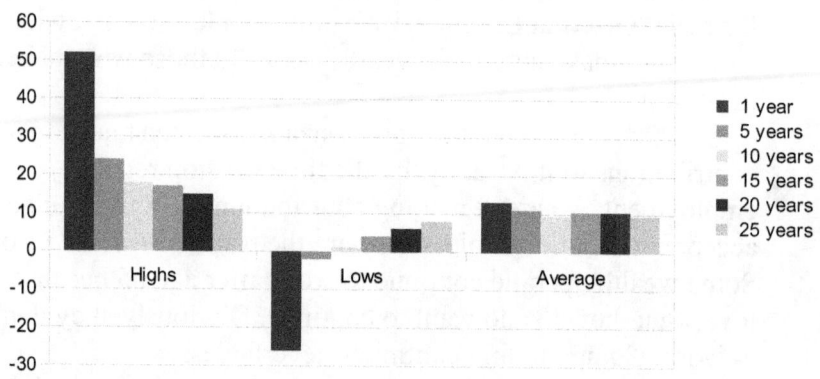

4

Automate monthly contributions to ensure success

One of the techniques for building wealth is to maintain consistent contributions to our **Wealth Reserve**™. This helps take our emotions out of the process of building wealth. If we do not watch the stock market or our account balance regularly, we will be less likely to panic. If we don't have to write and send the contribution each month, we won't stop investing when our account is down.

Our normal reaction to having money in an account is to watch it, guard it, think about how it is doing, compare its size and rate of growth. All of these actions are fine for a savings account. But as a silent partner in growing companies, this is not wise. We have to believe that global businesses will continue to grow. However, most people don't look at their wealth building in that way. Most people do not think of this account as a stake in many growing businesses. They sell as soon as they see their account go down. Client Tom, page 22, knew he only 'lost' if he sold shares.

One way we can help change our thinking is to try to put the account out of our immediate concern by making the contributions **automatic**. Like the Social Security contributions we make every payday, the contributions come out of our pay automatically. This can happen easily with a Roth 401k since our Plan administrator will deduct the amount we specify at Plan enrollment. In the same manner, we can have the Roth IRA trustee debit our checking account automatically every period.

As one client told me, "I never see the deduction, so I never miss it." Of course this client has already identified the $250 he has committed to his $1,000,000 future. He says that he would just waste the $250 anyway. He had been doing that for years because he never took the trouble to set his goals for short-term and long-term timelines. He took my advice and trimmed his spending on financial services. He used our Guides to find the $250 a month he was wasting on products and services he would never use or need. In Dan Keppel's amazon.com/Insiders-Guides-Discount-Financial-

Services/ you will find "tricks of the trade" that we insiders use to buy directly from quality manufacturers. Cut the middleman.

Many people have trouble keeping up the habit of investing every month. Some emergency always interupts this process. The delay in the periodic contributions causes the compounding effect to be reduced. The interruption is like starting the investment process late. This chart shows us what starting early or not putting off the investments can do. Over time, the delay compounds the lack of accumulation. Starting 5 years later means ending up with HALF the amount we were shooting for. It is hard to believe that missing that $250 a month for 5 years or $15,000 can reduce our total from $600,000 to $300,000. It's easy to say **I will start later**.

This is why our contributions to the account should not pass through our hands. We should have the money taken directly from our bank account by the trustee. Contributions are after-tax so you can take them, if necessary, with no tax payable. Nontaxable distributions from a Roth IRA won't affect your eligibility for student aid either. Later, in retirement, this money won't effect your Social Security benefits as of the rules today.

The second reason why this technique for developing wealth works is that when contributions are automatic, we do not have the temptation to try to time the market. Many people want to know the secret to timing the market so that they can invest right at the bottom of market cycles and sell at the peak of the market.

Unfortunately, it is a myth that we can do this all the time. Again, this is our misconception of how building wealth works.

Yes there are lucky gamblers. However, this is the exception. We are trying to build wealth over time. We want to end up with $1,000,000 tax-FREE. We are silent partners in building businesses that produce dividends and gains over time. We are not placing our contributions on red or black at the casino. We "hold forever."

Our account grows with steady contributions because in the month we buy $250 of company stocks in a mutual fund, we receive less shares when the price is high and more shares when the price is low. Studies have shown that this may result in buying shares at the least cost. You may invest a lump sum like your tax return all at once. However, it is not possible to know when the shares we buy will be at their lowest cost in the year.

Market timing is not possible. Consider how hard it is to find the lowest price at any given time in the market. There were ONLY <u>40 days</u> from 1950 to 2007 that produced 70% of all the S&P 500 index's total returns. That is <u>40 out of 14,528</u>. We can't possibly know when to buy into the businesses represented in the mutual fund we are using. We will lose money if we try to become traders who time the market. See John Bogle's analysis in <u>*Don't Count on It*</u>, p 169.

The key to building wealth is steady investing. Over time, stocks of growing companies have the most consistent record of providing 10-12% annual returns. We just don't know which companies and which time to invest are best. Luckily, we don't have to know. We need to understand the bigger picture.

The bigger picture is that we want our account to grow exponentially like Tom's (p. 22). We want to take advantage of the **miracle of compounding**. Since we don't have a million dollars, we are going to have to be patient to acquire it. We want every dollar we invest to count. We have $250-$500 a month to invest so we have to rely on consistent buying of shares to reach our goal.

Accumulations double in value every 8-10 years if we buy securities in the top two sectors (lines below). Of course the stock market doesn't move up at 10-12% EACH year. However, our wealth account will double and double and double so that by age 65, we could have over $1 million. Notice how the account values in the chart on page 22 for our client Tom move from $1 million to $2 million in 8 years, even with 3 years of losses. Of course, a million dollars will be worth less in the future because of inflation. But we will certainly appreciate our account values later no matter what our contributions are now. Consistency builds wealth.

Cumulative Wealth

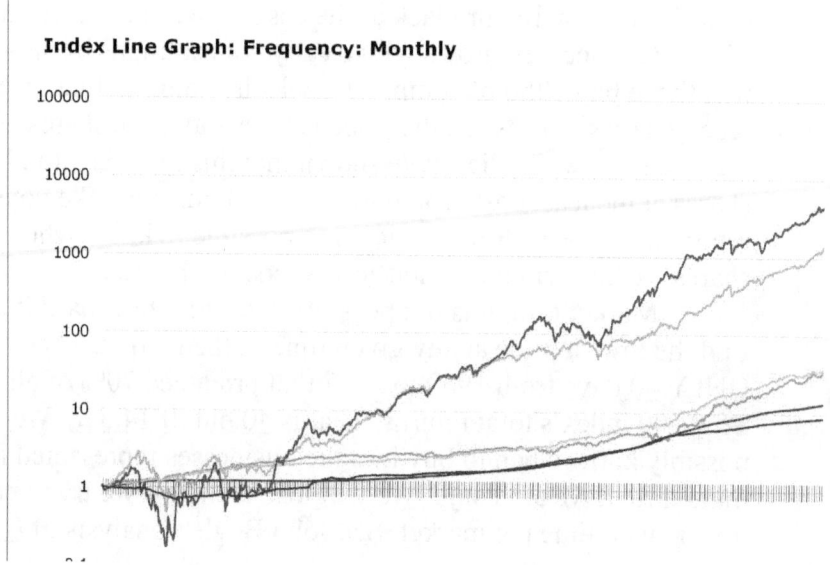

Index Line Graph: Frequency: Monthly

Top line—Small Cap Stocks
2nd line—Large Cap Stocks (S&P 500)
3rd line—US Long-term Corporate Bonds
4th line—Intermediate-term Government Bonds
5th line—US 30 day Government T-bills
6th line—US inflation

Courtesy: Dr. Campbell R. Harvey http://www.duke.edu/~charvey/

And the bonus of this geometric account growth is that it does not quit even after we stop adding our monthly contributions. Once the account has reached a certain mass, let's say after 20 years of contributions or $60,000, it will keep compounding. On page 32 we show you how this worked for contributions of $2,000 to a virtual account invested in the U.S. stock market (500 Index) over time. Some years we 'lose' 39%; some we 'gain' 38%.

We can see in the chart "Cumulative Wealth" above that over time, wealth accumulates at different rates depending on the type of assets we buy. For anyone who invested in smaller companies over any given 15 year period, the benefits were outstanding. For *each* $1,000 invested in 1940, $3,000,000 was the total return by the 1990's. Investing more cautiously in the large companies of the S&P 500, for instance, *each* $1,000 would have grown to almost a $1,000,00 by 2000. Yes, the lines are not perfectly straight, but growing $250 a month to $1,000,000 is definitely worth the ups and downs. Inflation is designated by the bottom line here. Putting all our money in a bank CD would accumulate at a rate represented by a line near that bottom line. If we sell, we really do lose.

Of course, these different rates of wealth accumulation assume two important factors—NO taxes and NO costs. We have eliminated the first killer of wealth—TAXES—by using a tax-FREE trust account. Costs of the investment type we use can also kill our total accumulations. My whole industry is built on the extraction of these costs from the accounts of investors. We must use low-cost stock funds to be successful investors.

Summary: Automate monthly contributions to ensure success.

One of the most difficult parts of building wealth is sticking with the program. If we put our monthly contributions on automatic, we will have no interruptions. If we instruct our trustee to debit our savings or checking account every month, we have a high probability of meeting our goals over time. We forget we are investing in our future and thus, we actually create one. Let the *Miracle of Compounding* work. Start automatic investing TODAY and become a millionaire!

$2,000 Annual Stock Market Investment 1950- '70- '80- '90- 2012

Year	Returns	Balance $2,000	Balance	Balance	Balance
1950	31%	$2,620			
1951	24%	$5,729			
1952	18%	$9,120			
1953	-1%	$11,009			
1954	52%	$19,773			
1955	31%	$28,523			
1956	5%	$32,049			
1957	-11%	$30,304			
1958	43%	$46,194			
1959	12%	$53,978			
1960	1%	$56,538			
1961	26%	$73,757			
1962	-8%	$69,697			
1963	24%	$88,904			
1964	16%	$105,449			
1965	12%	$120,342			
1966	-10%	$110,108			
1967	24%	$139,014			
1968	11%	$156,526			
1969	-8%	$145,844	2,000		
1970	4%	$153,757	2,080		
1971	14%	$177,563	4,651		
1972	19%	$213,681	7,915		
1973	-14%	$185,485	8,527		
1974	-26%	$138,739	7,790		
1975	37%	$192,813	13,412		
1976	24%	$241,568	19,111		
1977	-8%	$224,082	19,422		
1978	6%	$239,647	22,707		
1979	18%	$285,144	29,155	2,000	
1980	32%	$379,030	41,124	2,640	
1981	-5%	$361,978	40,968	4,408	
1982	22%	$444,053	52,421	7,818	
1983	21%	$539,724	65,850	11,879	
1984	6%	$574,228	71,921	14,712	
1985	32%	$760,621	97,575	22,060	
1986	19%	$907,519	118,494	28,632	
1987	5%	$954,995	126,519	32,163	
1988	17%	$1,119,684	150,367	39,971	
1989	32%	$1,480,623	201,125	55,402	2,000
1990	-3%	$1,438,144	197,031	55,680	1,940
1991	31%	$1,886,589	260,731	75,560	5,161
1992	8%	$2,039,676	283,749	83,765	7,734
1993	10%	$2,245,843	314,324	94,342	10,708
1994	2%	$2,292,800	322,651	98,268	12,962
1995	38%	$3,166,824	448,018	138,370	20,647
1996	23%	$3,897,654	553,522	172,656	27,856
1997	33%	$5,186,540	738,844	232,292	39,709
1998	28%	$6,641,331	948,281	299,894	53,387
1999	21%	$8,038,430	1,149,839	365,291	67,019
2000	-9%	$7,316,791	1,048,174	334,235	62,807
2001	-12%	$6,447,855	925,203	296,223	57,095
2002	-22%	$5,024,437	722,291	232,316	46,035
2003	29%	$6,459,474	930,787	301,119	61,730
2004	11%	$7,164,483	1,034,274	336,099	70,664
2005	5%	$7,512,677	1,084,540	352,433	74,098
2006	15%	$8,694,884	1,259,259	412,409	90,450
2007	5%	$9,163,538	1,327,133	434,638	95,325
2008	-39%	$5,601,431	813,388	268,074	60,754
2009	27%	$7,116,358	952,155	342,993	79,699
2010	15%	$8,186,112	1,097,278	396,742	93,954
2011	2%	$8,347,378	1,118,894	404,558	95,805
2012	16%	$9,666,264	1,295,679	468,478	110,942
Avg.	12%	12%	11%	13%	10%

Ibbotson Associates **Stocks average 11.4% per year, bonds 5%, CDs 3%.** Stocks have gone up as much as 54% and as low as –43% in 1 year, up to 28% or down to –12% in 5 years, up 20% or down 0% in 10 years, up 18% or up 3% in 20 years. Short term bonds have gone up 14% or up 0% in 1 year, up 11% or up 0% in 5 years, up 9% or up 0% in 10 years, up 10% or up 1% in 20 years.

5

Use low-cost mutual funds only

**"In every single time period and data point tested,
low-cost funds beat high-cost funds."**

According to an unbiased <u>Morningstar</u> study, low-cost funds beat
high-cost funds PERIOD. However, the myth of Wall Street is that
you must pay more for good performance. Not true. We all know
that in most groceries' prices, paying more (for packaging and TV
commercials) does not guarantee the best product.

The **best predictor** of your investing and wealth building
success is low cost. It is common sense that there are just too many
variables in the success of growing companies' stocks for anyone
to be able to pick them in advance on a consistent basis. A low-cost
stock mutual fund provides the best chance of maximizing our
accumulations as the market leaders change over time.

Contrary to Wall Street's hype, it does not matter which
stocks are rising or falling at any given time. If our account holds a
broad representation of stocks and our investment costs are low,
we will benefit over the long haul. We own them all!

Since the annual returns of stock funds have averaged 10-
12% over time, we want to pick the lowest cost mutual fund
available. A stock fund that reflects the overall market is called an
index fund. This kind of fund explained below costs only 0.05%
($5 per $10,000). Our account will compound at or near the 10-
12% over time since the costs are low compared to ones that
charge 1.5-2%. If we use the high-cost stock funds in our account,
we will earn about 8.5% over time. These funds pay managers high
salaries with expensive bonuses. The fund owners and sales staff
are paid well also. This is the cash cow of Wall Street.

The chart below makes it clear. Over time, the costs we pay
each year will cut our total accumulation by a THIRD or more.
Instead of compounding at 10-12% annually on average, some
people give up 1.5-2% of the earnings on their money to the
middle person. They end up with less.

Cost Matters: 0.19% v 1.68%

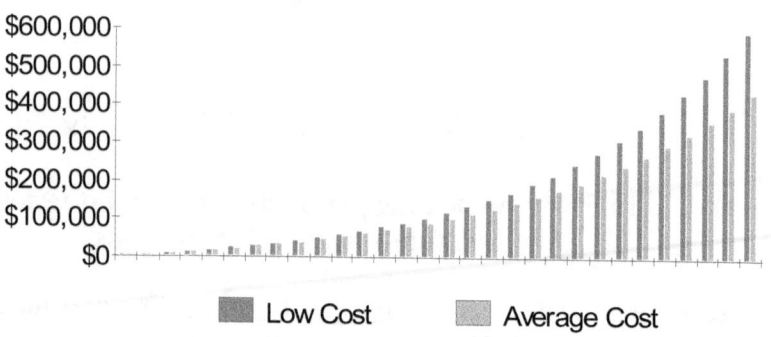

Wall Street says that we can earn more by paying a star manager to pick the right stocks on an ongoing basis. The money "experts" say we get what we pay for and a proven stock-picking manager will overcome the extra costs and make more for us.

You need to know that this myth has been proven wrong. The lowest cost funds don't pay a star manager and owner big bucks but come out ahead over time. There are simply too many variables for anyone or computer program to pick the winning stocks **all the time**. Some of the lowest cost funds are called index funds. When we buy an index, we are buying a piece of many companies that reflect the market. This gives us the same annual returns as the overall market over time. We pay tiny expenses.

Many studies have proven that index funds beat funds run by stock pickers most of the time. Low-cost <u>index funds</u> beat <u>86%</u> of funds with a stock-picking manager. *BusinessWeek* Apr 2009. <u>http://www.businessweek.com/investing/insights/blog/archives/200 9/04/where_have_all.html</u>.

When we investigate the experiences of the best money managers in the world, we find they recommend index funds to most people who invest as silent partners. Here are their statements:

Warren Buffett is probably history's greatest investor, in terms of results with $53 BILLION ($53 thousand million dollars) so far. He buys *companies* that provide valuable services to a great number of people. His company owns parts of Coke, GEICO, Fruit of the Loom, Benjamin Moore, Heinz, Burlington Northern, etc.

berkshirehathaway.com/
  He told Reuters:
"A very low-cost index is going to beat a majority of the amateur-managed money or professionally-managed money."

Compare the odds of selecting the correct mutual fund. A fund's chance of beating the market in EACH year is 3 out of 100.
nytimes.com/2009/02/22/your-money/stocks-and-bonds/22stra.html

Peter Lynch, brilliant manager, Magellan Fund "...you'd be just as well off if you'd invested in the S&P 500." *One Up on Wall Street*, 1989, p. 240.

Jonathan Clements, formerly ***The Wall Street Journal***
"Most people can do it themselves. ... By indexing, you don't just ensure that you will do better than most other investors. You will also enjoy the advantage of 'relative certainty.' . . . For most investors, Vanguard will be the place to go." *You've Lost It, Now What? How to beat the bear market and still retire on time*, 2003, p. 62, 70.

Charles D. Ellis, money managers' consultant
"The premise . . . that professional investment managers *can* beat the market . . . appears to be false. It is a loser's game. ... clients would have done better in a market fund." Returns are "splendidly predictable—on average and over time." *Investment Policy, How to Win the Loser's Game*, 1985, p. 5, 20, 34.

Jane Bryant Quinn, consumer advisor
"I'm a longtime booster of index mutual funds. These funds follow the market as a whole. Tons of research has shown that most money managers don't beat the markets they invest in, after costs. Maybe your own stocks or funds have excelled in the past couple of years. But in most cases, you've also been taking extra risk. The odds of superior performance are against you, in the long run. Indexing puts the odds on your side." *Los Angeles Business Journal*, May 8, 2000

Charles Schwab founder, discount broker
"I put my money where my mouth is: most of the mutual fund

investments I have are in index funds, approximately 75%. My core investments are index funds. Experienced investors have discovered that in any given year, on average, only 20 to 30 percent of mutual funds outperform the market. That is why I recommend index funds…"

Mr. Schwab tells of one of his friends who owned many well-run funds. After keeping track of all the dividends, taxes, reinvestments tax basis and statements, he found he earned the same return as the index of these funds. After selling them all, he bought the index fund. He has "what he wanted in the first place: diversification, tax advantages, one statement, and lower expenses." *Guide to Financial Independence*, 1998, pp. 90, 103, 111.

Motley Fool, Internet site about investing
"Almost **everything** that you will ever read about mutual funds beyond, "Buy an index fund." is superfluous to your long-term success in investing in mutual funds." Fool.com.

Walter Updegrave, senior editor, *Money*
"Mutual fund picking would be easier if there was one you could count on to outperform 70% or so of its competitors over long stretches of a decade or more. It's called an index fund. Although less than 10% of investors own an index fund, they are "one of the best-kept secrets" on Wall Street. My unabashed aim is to convince you to put at least a part of your money into one or more of these funds. You have a far less than a 50% chance of beating the market…. I strongly recommend that you make index funds your primary holding…." *The Right Way to Invest in Mutual Funds*, 1996, p 189-194.

Andrew Tobias, financial writer
"Scrimp and save, putting whatever you can into no-load, low-expense stock market index funds, both U.S. and foreign. You will do better than 80% of your friends and neighbors." *My Vast Fortune*, 1997, p. 158.

There are many books written on the subject of index and "managed" funds. If you wish to vanquish the hype and understand investing, skim *A Random Walk Down Wall Street* by Princeton University's Burton Malkiel. Here are the reasons why smart insiders use low-cost funds:

1. Both stock and bond index funds provide better returns than 86% of managed funds for periods greater than 10 years.
2. You earn more because you pay lower costs and taxes.
3. Low-cost funds build greater wealth over time.
4. Low-cost funds can be less volatile because they reflect whole sectors of the market.
5. Low-cost funds offer better diversification.
6. You know what you are paying for. No high-salary managers.
7. Low-cost funds don't require you to hope the manager will predict the future correctly. The odds of doing it are 1 in 15,000 each year separately. Over time, all funds provide average returns minus their costs.

> "Professional money management is a gigantic rip-off."
> Bill Gross, star bond manager, *Everything You've Heard About Investing is Wrong*

8. Low-cost funds are easy to buy.

Summary of many studies about index investing

First, fund managers try to predict the future of the market when they buy and sell securities in their funds. There is no proof this can be done well over time. Yesterday's winners are usually tomorrow's losers. The AVERAGE market return has been 10-12%, so a few managers will beat the average by luck—Just not the same ones every year. nytimes.com/2008/07/13/business/13stra.html
Second, the costs of the manager, their staff and operations must be paid for by you whether or not they earn you a dime. It is always better to pay as little as possible for the same performance. Costs can take 33% of your returns over time. Surprisingly, while the stock index rose 9%, investors with high paid managers averaged only **2.56%** annually from 1990-2010 (QAIB). DALBARinc.com.
Third, high cost managers get paid for increasing the size of their funds, not for making you rich. Bringing in more money is a full-time job. It is expensive to market the funds given that there are now thousands available. It is inevitable that popular funds will

grow until they produce average returns with high expenses. Managers want to be rich, not right.

Fourth, there is much less chance of you being treated poorly by fund management if the structure and governance are customer-oriented like Vanguard's and TIAA-CREF's are.

Fifth, many professional managers and Wall Street insiders place their core assets in low-cost index funds.

Summary: Use low-cost mutual funds only.

The best predictor of the success of a mutual fund is its cost. Usually the least expensive funds that match market averages beat the more expensive managed funds. Low-cost market index funds buy all the securities represented in a broad market. The goal of an index fund is to match its market. Low-cost index funds have provided returns that beat 80-90% of managed funds over the long-term. No manager has been able to predict the future so the returns regress to the mean—10-12%. The smart money is on the averages not the long shot. Buffett's Secret is the *Miracle of Compounding.* Low-cost funds maximize compounding.

"In every single time period and data point tested, low-cost funds beat high-cost funds."

6

Buy groups of stocks of growing companies worldwide

If we want to have a $1,000,000 tax-FREE account, we need a way to make it happen—a strategy. To be able to have a nest egg of $1 million requires that we know how and where to invest, invest regularly, invest properly, monitor accumulations along the way, and get help when we need it. We need a clear plan that takes only one hour to set up and only one hour per year to manage. Complicated plans just don't work for most people. Complicated strategies cost more to execute.

Picking *individual* stocks as a strategy is not likely to work for us. Professional managers and day traders have had limited success **over time**. Our strategy is to build wealth as a silent partner in growing global companies. Since it is unlikely that we (or anyone else) will be able to pick the next Google or Apple, we invest in a large group of firms. We do not need to fear picking the wrong one or picking one at the wrong time. As the founder of the largest mutual fund firm, John Bogle, says: "Don't look for the needle. Buy the haystack."

This is contrary to the myth of Wall Street 'professionals.' They make their living claiming to find the needle every year and we pay the price. Professionals promise that they can find the next big one and we pay them well because we want to be rich.

Like the lottery, we kid ourselves into thinking that "someone has to win, why not me." We don't believe we are wasting our money even though our rational mind knows that our chance of winning is low. Managed funds don't beat the market most of the time. The odds are like those of a lottery—18 million to 1. Like the lottery, when we invest in a managed fund to "beat the market" we don't count up the costs of the "tickets." We may buy $25 worth of tickets a week and end up winning $1,000 in a year. We spent $1,200 for $1,000.

In the same manner, a mutual fund manager advertises that

their fund has "beaten" the market and so we pay 1.5-2% of our assets every year. Over time we find that while the stock market index rose 10% from 1990-2010, we earned only 2.56% annually. This is what happened to retail investors according to Dalbar's QAIB recent study. DALBARinc.com

Some of us keep switching to the hot funds according to the advertising we see every month. Some are always chasing the last most successful mutual fund. Some buy the fund at the high point because they want the winner. They sell the fund when it falls and they want the next high flier. Over time they never earn the return promised by the manager.

In this way, costs can take 40% of their returns over time. Each time they sell and buy, they give up earnings and perhaps part of their money if they use a sales person charging 5%. Even if they stay with one managed mutual fund that has annual fees of 1.5-2%, they are killing the miracle of compounding.

Using the compounding calculator, we can see that our accumulation drops to $.7 million if we earn 10% instead of 11.5% annually. We could have $1 million in 33 years at 11.5%. http://www.moneychimp.com/calculator/compound_interest_calcul ator.htm

Another Wall Street myth is that investing in market index funds will produce average (mediocre) returns. It is true that the returns will be close to the returns of the market. However, historically the market returns are the ones that are somewhat predictable. Investing in growing companies provides no guaranteed return but the average returns have held steady since the 1950s. See page 32.

Wall Street history is littered with strategies that were said to beat the market. The brilliant stock pickers have also come and gone. Today, though, which one of the new ones are we going to invest with? No one knows. The ONLY thing we really know is that the averages of broad market indexes have produced 10-12% on average each year.

For example, some of my clients use these Vanguard mutual funds which have earned over 11% for a long time. Of course, there is no guarantee of future returns, but they have all done fairly well. Most started with the 500 Index and added companies in the Energy, Health and International sectors. These 10 funds have done well over time. Many investors pick Vanguard funds because the funds are well run "at cost." No "bells and whistles." No expensive managers and overhead. No owner taking profits from our investment returns.

2011 Total Return	Fund	Long-term Return*	Longevity
1.97%	500 Index	10.36%	since 1976
-1.74%	Energy	12.71%	since 1984
-3.73%	Extended Market	9.96%	since 1987
11.45%	Health	16.30%	since 1984
-13.68%	International Growth	10.50%	since 1981
-1.84%	PRIMECAP	12.79%	since 1984
-2.80%	Small Cap Index	10.26%	since 1960
9.63%	Wellesley Income	10.16%	since 1970
-4.00%	Windsor	11.00%	since 1958
2.70%	Windsor II	10.18%	since 1985
0.00%	Average	11.42%	

*Average Annual Returns as of 12/31/11.

My clients are long-term investors, not speculators. They believe that investments in low-cost funds (index and managed) are their best chance of reaching their goals. They have been rewarded for that belief. Vanguard has many low-cost funds and their service is better than most funds.

Remember, we are investing for the long-term. Most pension funds are invested in stock and bond indexes. Even though the market fell 22% in 2002 and rose 29% in 2003, the average was still holding. Average returns mean we do not suffer the lowest lows or the highest highs. They return to the average: 10-12%.

Most of the largest growing companies in the world are held by these funds. Large US firms are now earning at least half of their profits overseas so we are benefiting from growth around the world. This is important because we don't want to miss important earnings progress as the developing nations like China and India expand their economies.

We don't know exactly which companies will be winners but we want to participate in all of them. We want to own some smaller growing companies too. If they become successful, they will move to the large company funds. We are exposed to almost all areas of the global economy by buying shares of these mutual funds at the lowest cost. We suffer the ups and downs of the markets just like every investor. However, we see that some funds do better at certain times while others do worse. Together we see clients hitting their goal of 10-12% average annual returns.

This type of investing has the greatest chance of avoiding severe swings in the overall accumulation. This type of strategy—investing in different types and sizes of companies in different sectors around the world—is called Modern Portfolio Theory.

Modern Portfolio Theory

Some clients use the MPT strategy to control risk while increasing returns. MPT (Moneychimp.com/articles/risk/riskintro.htm) holds that if we put our eggs in different baskets of assets that grow at different times, then the value of all our eggs grows with fewer ups and downs. We can manage the ups and downs of equity funds by buying different ones over time. Higher risk assets are small caps, REITs and foreign stocks. This strategy may earn 10-12% with less volatility.

Members assemble different asset classes (see http://www.callan.com/research/download/?file=periodic%2ffree%2f655.pdf) that fit their risk-reward tastes. According to this Nobel Prize-winning strategy moneychimp.com/articles/risk/portfolio.htm, a high return asset with a low correlation to other assets in the portfolio can actually reduce the volatility of the whole. It may be possible to earn high returns with less risk **overall** as each asset goes up and down at different times. See the example at fool.com/personal-finance/retirement/2007/03/06/5-steps-to-salvage-your-retirement.aspx.

The past provides only PROBABLE futures. But isn't $1,000,000 (plus or minus $100,000) better than $140,000. Your $250-per-month deposit in the bank for 33 years will be worth about $140,000 after tax compared with about $1 million from stock investing with no tax. Every investor would be better off with $1 million (+/- $100,000) than $140,000 from a bank.

When clients begin investing, they cannot buy all 10 Vanguard funds at once with $250 per month. Vanguard has minimums on all funds so they can keep their expenses low for everyone.

There are two ways to start our **Wealth Reserve**™. The

easiest way is to save $250 a month in our savings account until we have the $1,000 minimum for Vanguard's entry fund: STAR #56. We can open the Roth IRA by phone or online: STAR minimum is $1,000. Most Vanguard funds need $3,000 to start. We can keep contributing to this index fund until we have $3,000 for the 500 Index and then $3,000 for the Extended Market funds. Vanguard is at 800.551.8631.

The second way to begin is to open a Roth IRA at TIAA-CREF, the world's largest pension company, primarily for educational and research institutions. Low expenses and low initial contributions ($100) make TIAA-CREF an organization we can stay with for life. TIAA-CREF 800.842.2888.

At TIAA-CREF.org, we can make application and begin immediately with an automatic monthly contribution of $100 or more from our bank account. We can follow how the assets grow by themselves. TIAA-CREF has two funds that provide us with the diversity of companies worldwide: TIAA-CREF Equity Index and TIAA International Equity.

Request a prospectus (owner's manual) for each fund you will be using at Vanguard or TIAA-CREF. Both mutual fund firms have experienced salaried representatives that provide accurate information about accounts and funds. Both offer low-cost index funds that hold a broad representation of the market returns of 10-12%. This is a building block for accumulating wealth.

Both firms are focused on you, not on profits.

Summary: Buy groups of stocks of growing companies worldwide.

This strategy provides long-term growth of 10-12% annually on average with the benefit of avoiding single company or industry failures. It provides exposure to new growth potential around the world with less risk than holding one company, one sector, or one country stocks. This gives us asset diversification since no one knows what the future may bring. You become a millionaire without the emotional turmoil of stock picking/timing.

It is the amount we KEEP that matters!

Cost matters!
10-year returns, all equity funds

Legend: Low-cost quartile, High-cost quartile

	Actual return*	Risk-adjusted return	After-tax return*
Low-cost quartile	10.2%	10.3%	8.3%
High-cost quartile	6.8%	6.5%	4.3%

*Source: Morningstar avg. ann. returns for 10 yrs ended 8/03.

7

Spend less than you earn

If we don't have a $3,000 tax refund, we need to find at least $250 per month to invest in order to build our $1 million **Wealth Reserve**™. We can build wealth by following the Buffett strategy, but we need to have at least $250 available to put to work. In my experience, it doesn't matter how much people earn, most say they don't have the $250 a month to invest for their future. "Today is hard enough," they complain.

Yes, that may well be, but if we don't find the $250 we won't have a very happy tomorrow. We have to go back to our goal. We want to build wealth: accumulating $1,000,000 over time. Based on the way wealth **compounds**, we need to identify at least $250 a month on a permanent basis. Earl Crawley started with dimes. http://www.youtube.com/watch?v=XD0svDGyLWU

Budget is a dirty word so we won't use it. No one wants to be restricted in their spending. Even the people who know they are wasting $100 a month on the lottery, still play. I know it satisfies an immediate riches fantasy. I know because I used to play every week like many others who never saw the power of compounding.

I want to explain how we can find the $250 a month to invest from a different perspective. If we are going to spend all of our income, we need to adopt a "spending plan" with the $250 a month for investment included in it. Otherwise, we won't accumulate $1,000,000. Even if we don't have 33 years, our $250 could grow to a significant sum. See the compounding chart:

Monthly	Accumulation at 12% per year									
	5	10	15	20	25	30	35	40	45	50
$100	$8,167	$23,004	$49,958	$98,925	$187,884	$349,496	$643,095	$1,176,477	$2,145,469	$3,905,834
$200	$16,334	$46,008	$99,916	$197,850	$375,768	$698,992	$1,286,190	$2,352,954	$4,290,938	$7,811,668
$300	$24,501	$69,012	$149,874	$296,775	$563,652	$1,048,488	$1,929,285	$3,529,431	$6,436,408	$11,717,502
$500	$40,835	$115,020	$249,790	$494,625	$939,420	$1,747,480	$3,215,475	$5,882,385	$10,727,346	$19,529,169

A spending plan is just a way to set priorities for our regular spending. During our working lives, we earn between $1.5 and $2.5 million before taxes. We can accumulate another $1 million to accomplish all that we want to do in life by using a small part of that income to buy assets that "grow by themselves."

Using a Spending Plan is **like brushing your teeth**—it's a habit that isn't that difficult to learn—then it is automatic. If we want our plan to become a habit, we have to practice it. If we consciously spend our income on those items on our priority list, we can't fail to develop the habit. We are teaching ourselves that we can have whatever we want in time. We are not saying "no" to that desire. We are saying put it on our list. We will get what we want eventually.

First, our Spending Plan must include what we need to function. Our future is part of our immediate needs in the sense that if we don't prepare now, we won't have the future we want. Again, building a $1,000,000 **Wealth Reserve**™ is a lifelong process and requires making a commitment. Like building a business, it takes planning and following the steps we talked about so far. And the miracle of compounding.

There are a number of ways to identify the $250 a month we need to build our future. Some clients include the $250 in their automatic bill payment or have the trustee debit their account automatically. The contribution is just another bill like rent, mortgage, utilities, car payment, cable, phone, etc. They live on the balance of their income.

Others set up family goals and decide to put a certain amount in a separate account for each goal. In this way, they keep the wealth building process in the forefront of their monthly bill payments ritual. Whatever way works for you. The important part is changing the status of wealth building from a vague future to a monthly priority.

Most clients find that the easiest way is to set up an automatic debit of their checking account by the trustee at the time of the application for the Roth IRA. If we are using a Roth 401k or other employer account, we set up the retirement account with automatic contributions. Some use their tax refund every year.

The Spending Plan idea works for all types of goals: college fund, emergency fund, vacation fund, new car fund, business start-up fund, whatever we decide to put at the top of our list of priorities. If we don't have this list, we can make one easily.

Clients who are successful have made written plans in some form or other. They have some idea of how much they will need at some time in the future. For short-term goals we can use our savings account but for long-term goals we need to use higher return securities. Many clients have trouble deciding which investment to use for each goal.

I explain the chart we displayed on page 12 above. Stock mutual funds are the investment of choice for any long-term accumulation goal. As per the chart, annual returns of 10-12% are the norm for any accumulation over 10-15 years. Once we build up a sizable balance in a long-term account, we can "borrow" from ourselves for short-term needs as long as we pay ourselves back.

Thus, clients have used their long-term accumulation **Wealth Reserve**™ for vacations, cars, appliances, emergencies, etc. This works if they pay themselves back. The **Wealth Reserve**™ is set up as a Roth IRA so the *contributions* are not taxed when used before age 59.5. After that age, there are no taxes at all—NEVER. However, to meet our long-term goals, we have to pay ourselves back quickly so compounding can continue.

Another benefit of using a Spending Plan is that we become focused on how we spend our money. We are more inclined to buy only what we need. For most of us, when we shop for groceries, we seek to get the most for our money by shopping for discounts and by buying in bulk. In the last ten years, the financial services industry has started to offer better values on products with discounts. We can avoid overpaying the middle people and buying products we really don't need.

How do we know? The Insiders Guides provide an easy way to save $3,000 or more on financial products we already use. There are buyer's guides for each specific area. We review some of the ways to find $250 in savings in the next chapter.

Summary: Spend less than you earn.

We can't build wealth by spending more than we earn. Building wealth takes patience and commitment to investing every month. Some people don't try to be disciplined investors. They let the trustee debit the $250 every month so they can't fail to invest. Continuous investing allows the *Miracle of Compounding* to happen.

Are you paying too much?

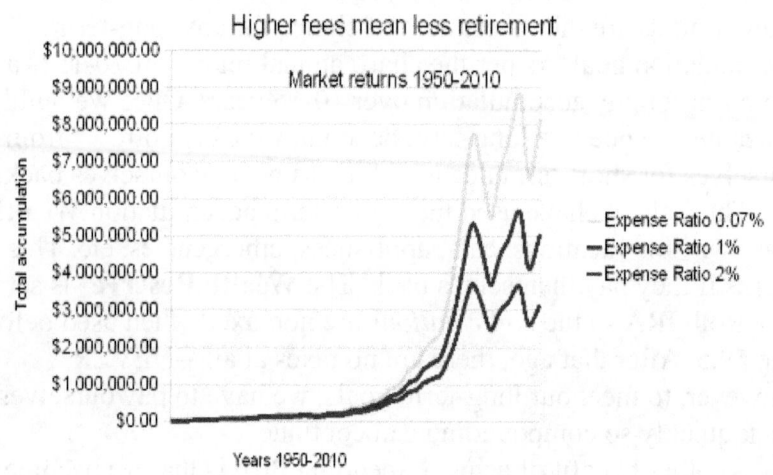

Higher fees mean less retirement

Market returns 1950-2010

Total accumulation

$10,000,000.00
$9,000,000.00
$8,000,000.00
$7,000,000.00
$6,000,000.00
$5,000,000.00
$4,000,000.00
$3,000,000.00
$2,000,000.00
$1,000,000.00
$0.00

Years 1950-2010

Expense Ratio 0.07%
Expense Ratio 1%
Expense Ratio 2%

8

Buy only the products you need—save $3,000 a year

It is easy to build wealth if we already have a pile of money. It takes 6-9 years to accumulate $1 million if you already have $500,000. But how do we capture that first $50,000, $100,000 or $250,000? It comes from buying assets that 'grow by themselves.' It takes time and the easiest way to make sure we reach our goal is to make our monthly contributions automatic.

But where do we get the $250 a month to invest? The best way is to "REDIRECT" the **cash we already spend** on things we really don't need or can buy for less.

Monthly	Accumulation at 12% per year									
	5	10	15	20	25	30	35	40	45	50
$100	$8,167	$23,004	$49,958	$98,925	$187,884	$349,496	$643,095	$1,176,477	$2,145,469	$3,905,834
$200	$16,334	$46,008	$99,916	$197,850	$375,768	$698,992	$1,286,190	$2,352,954	$4,290,938	$7,811,668
$300	$24,501	$69,012	$149,874	$296,775	$563,652	$1,048,488	$1,929,285	$3,529,431	$6,436,408	$11,717,502
$500	$40,835	$115,020	$249,790	$494,625	$939,420	$1,747,480	$3,215,475	$5,882,385	$10,727,346	$19,529,169

While working with clients, I have found that most of us waste $3,000 or more each year on financial services. The average loan we make to the IRS (tax refund) is $3,022. We can stop paying for services we don't need. This takes a little thought and questioning on our part, but in reality it is the same process as buying any commodity. When we buy groceries, do we buy the house brand or the one on sale or the one we see advertised?

On a little bigger scale, do we buy the new car advertised with a new "push" starter as opposed to an old key-type ignition? Do we pay an extra $1000 to buy the one with a screen to tell us where to go or just buy a map? The difference between paying full price for a new car and a 3 year old model with fewer gadgets can be 40% or more. When we put our future on top of our priority list, we can REDIRECT the savings to a more worthwhile purpose.

It is the same with financial services. Most of us are not used to shopping for insurance, mutual funds, banking and mortgages. So we don't. We are operating under the mythology of Wall Street —'professionals' say we need them to help guide us, for a price. But we don't need them anymore. The world has changed.

Let's take some examples of **annual savings**:

Auto insurance: save $400 or more EVERY year by changing/dropping some features we don't need.

Home insurance: save $200 or more EVERY year by changing one limit.

Life insurance: save $1,000 or more EVERY year by using direct to consumer insurer.

Mutual funds: save $2-3,000 EVERY year by using low-cost providers.

Bank: save $120 EVERY year by using a low-cost provider of the benefits we usually use.

Mortgage: save $2,000 on closings and lower interest rates.

Investments: earn 15-30% guaranteed just by paying off credit cards.

Tax refund: save the average $3,022 by *paying* in April.

Using the Insiders' Guides put together by Dan Keppel in his book *The Insiders' Guides to Buying Discount Financial Services: Buy Direct and Save $3,000 Every Year,* we can REDIRECT the $250 a month without having to give up anything. We don't need to tighten our belt or make a budget. We can give up things we would not benefit from anyway. http://theinsidersguides.com/

Dan gave me a number of testimonials from people who have told him about their experience using the Guides.

George B. New York:
"I saved $1,356 on my vehicle insurance using your Insider's Guide to Vehicle Insurance. I saved by using some of your Insiders' 'tricks of the trade' like dropping the extras that I already had."

John D. New York:
"I canceled my life insurance and used the money to buy the mutual funds. You were right. I didn't need the insurance anymore. My kids are all grown. My new wife and I invest as much as we can now. Your Guide to 'Living' Insurance is a great way to look at our insurance needs."

Mark K. Ohio:
"I had no idea how to invest in the 401k that my new job offered. I have not been disappointed with the mutual funds suggested by other members. I saved about a $1,000 by transferring my old 401k mutual funds to the low-cost funds in your Guide. When I sold my primary residence in 2004, I followed members' advice with the gains. I use all your Guides to help me save more for my retirement since I got a late start. Thanks."

Dan has a great example of the big savings we can expect by shopping for insurance. Dan found that people usually pick name brands instead of shopping for services they need. Companies spend a lot for TV advertising and gimmicks.

Example:

MetLife charged $983 for a $300,000 30-year **term policy**. This same $300,000 benefit was sold by Savings Bank Life Insurance for $384 a year. Their financial strength ratings are A+ and their underwriting requirements are the same. The difference, $599, over 30 years is $17,970. If invested, this difference can add $175,000 to OUR **Wealth Reserve**™.

Most people are amazed at the difference a little research and shopping can accomplish. Even if we did not have Dan's Guide, a search of the Internet would reveal several portals that quote rates. Unfortunately, most people don't take the time to shop or don't know exactly what they need. The Guide helps us make the decision of where to shop and what to buy.

Summary: Buy only the products you need—save $3,000 a year.

Buying only what we need in every financial service area will provide the cash for contributions. **We give up nothing and gain our future**. Taking the time to shop in each area of our expenses helps us make our future happen. Shopping for an hour can add $175,000 to our account. Yes, it is worth it! Wasting money robs you of the Miracle of Compounding. *Compounding makes you a millionaire from your Gold Mine*.

The Roth IRA Rules

Contributions:

$5,500 ($6,500 over age 50) each year
Income under $127,000 (2013) single
married $188,000 (2013)

Distributions:

Tax-FREE for contributions.
And Tax-FREE for earnings if
Over age 591/2,
Account open 5 years,
Earnings are taxable unless
Disabled,
First home ($10,000),
Death

Bonus:

Account can grow tax-FREE for life
Distribution rules don't apply
Heirs don't pay income tax
Account has no maximum

Check with your tax preparer
www.IRS.gov/pub/irs-pdf/p590.pdf

9

Manage the account *only* once a year

"We continue to make more money when *snoring* than when active." Warren Buffett, Berkshirehathaway.com/

This is the advice of the most successful investor of our day. He is making it clear that we should NOT touch our investments very often. Contrary to the advice of the Wall Street 'professionals,' he leaves his assets alone to compound over time. He does not follow the 'hot' investment of the day. He buys the stock of growing companies around the world. He has held some investments for over 40 years.

Our emotions tell us to sell when our account balance goes down. We want to buy the next big investment to make up for previous losses. This is why we have a hard time following Buffett's advice. However, the emotions that cause us to be bad investors are what we can control—not the stock price of growing companies worldwide.

Our contributions to our **Wealth Reserve**™ need to be automatic so we buy more shares when the market is down and less when it is up. This helps us control our emotions. When the market is down, we need to look at the line graph on page 16. We don't know when the market will be up or down but we see that if we sell, we may miss the next advance. This is why we have to remember Warren Buffett's advice and hold on to stocks. In fact, Mr Buffett says "**our favorite holding period is forever.**" http://www.berkshirehathaway.com/letters/1988.html

When we own a broad cross-section of the market, we really don't have to worry about buying and selling our mutual funds. There is no better investment for the long term. Besides, what would we buy if we sold? We have seen that stocks are the safest investment for periods over 10 years.

We believe that the only way to avoid bad investment decisions is to NOT make any investment decisions in haste. Stick with the idea that we only have to look at our tax-FREE account once a year. At that time, I make sure I am making contributions to the specific mutual fund I need to build in order to keep them equally funded. Set it and forget it.

For instance, when I first started investing, I used the 500 Index. After I had accumulated enough to buy the Extended Market, I sold shares of 500 Index ($3,000) and bought it. I kept investing into the 500 Index until I had the minimum for the next one on the list. I repeated this pattern until I had the minimum in each. Then I picked one to add $250 a month for one year. The next year, I did the same until I completed the list again and again.

Today, I am still making contributions using the same rotation. Once a year, I compare the total account balance to where I think it should be. I note what happened during the year for any one fund. I go to the Vanguard site and read about that fund. Do I need to make a change? No, I don't. I only use the 10 funds listed above. They have done well consistently over the years.

Notice that when we buy each fund at first, we have to sell shares in the 500 Index to do so. Because we are using a Roth IRA, there is **no tax** on this sale if the share price has gone up. Also, each year, our dividends are re-invested without paying tax on that income. This is part of the miracle of compounding. Our account is growing without taxes each year. Any other non-retirement account would be diminished by the tax paid each year.

There is no need to sell funds that have done well in order to re-balance the 10 funds' balances equally. Most of the research shows that re-balancing each year does NOT improve the long-term outcome of the whole portfolio. Some clients use their contributions each year to add to the fund that has grown the least. However, as each fund becomes larger, the effect of adding contributions becomes smaller over time.

When we have to sell shares to meet an emergency or avoid interest payments by using cash for large ticket items, we may sell shares in each fund by equal dollar amounts. This is a better strategy than selling shares in only one fund since we don't know which fund may recover the fastest going forward. In the same way as accumulating shares, we need to reimburse our account for the amount used. It is very desirable to also continue to make contributions at the regular rate--$250 per month. This way we are assured of catching up to our position as we reach our goal.

However, we found that after accumulating a large proportion of our goal, adding the $250 per month did not seem to matter to the outcome. For instance, our client whose account is shown on page 22 took $25,000 for a used luxury car in the year the account hit over half a million. He also stopped making contributions. His account total did not suffer long term.

Actually this client redirected his $250 monthly contribution to his grandchild's **Wealth Reserve**™ so that they might have a financial foundation all their life. If he keeps giving this $3,000 a year to his offspring for 40 years, they could have $2,000,000 by age 50. The grandchild "earns" $3,000 a year doing odd jobs for him. Learn more about this "Gift of a Lifetime" in Dan Keppel's book, amazon.com/Give-your-Grandchild-000-Lifetime/.

Summary: Manage the account only once a year.

Our tax-FREE account does not require us to hire an advisor to manage it. Advisors do not know what the future holds anymore than we do so paying them 1-3% each year just reduces our annual returns. Their fees/charges can take up to 40% of our total possible accumulations over time. We are investing for the long term and there is no proof that switching from one fund to another during the year does anything to help our results. As we add more contributions, we can rotate through each fund we use. The less we tamper with our fund balances the better our experience will be. Buffett's method is to hold investments forever. That enables the *Miracle of Compounding* to work.

Your Action Plan

This week:
Goal

_____

_____

This month:
Goal

_____

_____

_____

_____

This year:
Goals

_____

_____

_____

_____

_____

_____

_____

_____

_____

_____

_____

_____

10

Spend $250,000 tax-FREE income

We have put the **Miracle of Compounding** to work in our Gold Mine with $9 a day "expenses." We have learned to be patient and accumulate $250,000 or more. We have paid back any amounts that we borrowed to pay cash for large purchases or deductibles. We have been fortunate that the historical averages of market returns have produced the accumulations we set as our goals.

NOW WHAT?

If we are over age 59.5, we can spend the account each year and pay no income taxes. As of 2013, most states follow the IRS code on our **Wealth Reserve**™, a Roth IRA—§ 408 trust account. There are exceptions for taking money early and spending contributions: http://www.irs.gov/retirement/article/0,,id=137307,00.html

Some clients have moved some of their accumulations into a bond fund in order to provide a monthly check to their checking account for their regular expenses. They created a retirement spending plan that assured them of that monthly income of a fixed dollar amount with this Guide. amazon.com/Your-Retirement-Spending-Plan-enough

We may want to create a $1,000,000 nest egg in order to provide the same buying power as we have today because of inflation. I am assuming that most families will need at least $50,000 a year to live on in retirement. We don't know what will happen to Social Security by 2033. We don't know what employer pensions might look like by then. I am assuming that inflation will continue at a 3% rate. It might be more or less. I have no idea. However, we must prepare for inflation.

At 3%, inflation will make the goods we buy now for $50,000 cost about $80,000. This is not exact. I don't know what will happen in 40 days let alone 40 years. If Social Security or employer pensions can add to our basic income, that is fine. But we don't want to count on them.

I am using $50,000 as a basic needs income because that has been my experience of what working people desire. It is also an amount that could be generated by a $1,000,000 account balance. Many clients use 6-8% as a target for their investment returns in retirement. This is just an approximation of the average returns over time.

Some clients move half their balances into a bond or balanced fund in order to generate the income for the coming year. The balance of their account remains in the broad stock funds we have listed above. These funds will continue to produce returns in the 10-12% range. If there is a bad year like 2008, we are not taking money out of our principal at a bad time. We take the money from a bond fund like the Vanguard Total Bond which has traditionally been less volatile.

The funds we have listed above include some of the most consistent low volatility returns over time. The Wellesley Income fund has produced over 10% per year on average since 1970 with few losses. It contains stocks and bonds. **This fund alone might be our source** of annual withdrawals of principal, interest and dividends. Since this account is not taxable, there are no tax considerations in the decision of which fund to tap for our monthly income.

Because we have no tax liability on this income of 8% per year, we may not have to pay tax on our other income like Social Security and/or our qualified retirement funds. Up to 85% of Social Security benefits are currently subject to federal income taxes. The IRS worksheet determines the percentage based on all our other income. Typically those with little or no other income currently have no tax due on their Social Security benefits. Pensions are taxed as income since we did not pay tax on the contributions.

If we have reached $1 million, we will pay little income tax on our income in retirement since 8%, $80,000 ($50,000 adjusted for inflation) will be tax-FREE. This will give us up to 30% more cash to spend compared with others who do not have the **Wealth Reserve**™. Pensions and other taxable income may be taxed at even higher rates in the future to pay for the two wars, two bank bailouts and two tax cuts that we endured since 2001. We have never gone to war and taken tax breaks at the same time before so this will take time to work out. Rates may go up in the future.

Our tax-FREE income will provide us with our basic-needs

income and if we continue to follow the same 10 steps of building wealth, we will find a comfortable lifestyle throughout the 30 to 40 years of not working unless we want to.

I and many clients are assuming we will work at least part time after we take full retirement and begin collecting Social Security. If benefits are cut, we will need to work. We are encouraged to use our tax-FREE income to develop a small business since this can help us control the income that is taxed.

As I mentioned at the beginning of this book, many working millionaires are self-employed. Running a small business is a great way to control the taxes we pay. Taxes are the biggest killer of wealth building that exists. It destroys the compounding factor.

The accumulation of $250,000 or more over time can be achieved with patience and perseverance. Spending the income that our Gold Mine can generate may require us to plan our spending. If we use the same 10 steps of wealth building to prepare for retirement, we will probably have enough to take care of long-term health care and other unforeseen expenses. Since we don't know what may happen, we will want to continue the same habits we have developed before retirement. We live within our means.

We may find that we will have a sizable legacy as we age. There are many ways to pass on our wealth that don't require an attorney on contingency or complicated legal formulations. Many clients have found that incremental gifts to charity and family provide immediate gratification. They have used the suggestions for wealth transfer Dan Keppel presented in the *Retirement Spending Plan*.

Summary: Spend $250,000 tax-FREE income.

This money is tax-FREE. It has more purchasing power than regular income. Working millionaires typically don't go out and buy a mansion and the trappings of the wealthy when they retire. They usually have paid off their homes. They travel and share with family and friends. Some continue to earn income doing what they enjoy or provide help to others in their volunteer efforts. Now we can enjoy $250,000 or more from our *Hidden Gold Mine*.

How to Buy Securities For Retirement

1. Cost matters: Broker/advisor cost 1% to 3%

   If you use a salesperson, fees can cost HALF A NEST EGG!
      $3,000 per year @12% for 33 years = $1,127,324
      $3,000 per year @12-1% for 33 years = $887,525
      $3,000 per year @12-2% for 33 years = $702,083
      $3,000 per year @12-3% for 33 years = $558,284

2. Broker/advisor stock picking does not beat index funds over the long run. No money manager has been able to beat the market consistently. No one can forecast the future.

3. Time is the key to investment success. The chance of you buying AND selling, both, at the right times, is near zero.

4. A Tax-FREE investment account increases your balance 30%. Avoid federal, state, local, DI, FUTA, SUTA, FICA, MED, etc etc.

5. Putting all your money in one stock or market sector guarantees failure over time. No one investment is perfect.

6. 'Dollar cost average' buying technique lowers the cost of shares over time. When you invest a fixed amount each month, you buy more mutual fund shares when the price is low and less when high. Over time, you will own more shares at a lower average cost.

7. $9 a day uncovers **Your Hidden Gold Mine**.

Conclusion

Just think if you had started earlier

$250,000 or more tax-FREE is in your **Gold Mine**.
What did you do with your refund this year? Most of us can't remember. Just think if you had started mining earlier.

In my experience with clients, most have been able to use the steps of building wealth to accumulate $250,000, then $1,000,000 by themselves. Some have asked for help. They did not need stock-picking skills. They did not need to use individual stocks or high-cost mutual funds offered by a sales person.

Many of these folks just needed confirmation of their own thinking. They made the decisions but wanted to be sure there was nothing they were missing. The industry has made building wealth a mystery so that they can tell us we need them: a well-paid "doctor" of financial health. The industry takes $560 billions from investors' accounts year after year with limited improvement. Frequent trading in the account usually does NOT benefit us.
pbs.org/moyers/journal/09282007/

On the other hand, if a person is paying 1-3% of their nest egg every year for an advisor, they expect to get something for their money. Most advisors need over $250,000 in an account to make it worth their time. That is $5,000 a year in fees which the firm splits with them 2/3-1/3. As we pointed our earlier, over time that fee goes up as our balance goes up and can take up to 40% of our total possible accumulation.

The key to reaching our goal of $1,000,000 is compounding of high returns over time. If we pay 2% to get 10-12%, we net 8-10%. Since we know that no advisor can guarantee 10-12% and most studies show investing directly without a "professional" can yield a better result, there is no reason to give up 2%. Advisors usually charge 2% whether they beat the averages or not so it is better to go for the 10-12% on our own. Advisors don't give refunds!!

The clear winning strategy is to use the Buffett Investment Secret and let compounding work its miracle. Over time using a tax-FREE account without an advisor fee, we can accumulate

$1,000,000 from $250 a month at 10-12%. Using a calculator http://www.moneychimp.com/calculator/compound_interest_calculator.htm, we find the range is 32 to 36 years. If we and our spouse each have an account, we can shorten the time—perhaps 27 years.

If we use an advisor, we may give up over $300,000 in total accumulation. That assumes we earn an average of 10%, the best possible case. Research has shown that the average brokerage investor actually earns about **2.56%** annually. 1990-2010 (QAIB) DALBARinc.com. Brokers encourage selling to buy the hot one.

Our **Gold Mine** produces because we use a straightforward strategy—compounding—AND a unique tax-FREE trust account that eliminates the biggest killer of wealth: TAXES. We have seen that compounding over time is the real engine for building wealth. Most people are NOT going to be successful at this because they have no patience to let their money dig the gold.

We can be our own masters of wealth with patience. There is no need to pick stocks or hire expensive advisors or product pushers with hidden fees. We can do it ourselves if we consider the process as a business. Our plan works for those who work it. The plan is the following 10 steps:

1. Create a tax-FREE account.
2. Use a tax-favored account for lifetime savings.
3. **Compound** high earnings over time.
4. Automate monthly contributions to ensure success.
5. Use low-cost mutual funds only.
6. Buy groups of stocks of growing companies worldwide.
7. Spend less than you earn.
8. Buy only the products you need—save $3,000 a year.
9. Manage the account only once a year.
10. Spend $250,000 tax-FREE income.

I won't be calling you. You must take the first step. I don't have a product to sell you. You have to call Vanguard or TIAA-CREF yourself to set up your FREE account. It takes about an hour to set up a Roth IRA for each of you. You can do it online or by phone. If you don't have your tax refund, you can begin with TIAA-CREF and $100 automatic contributions or Vanguard with $1,000. Put the contributions on automatic so you don't have to decide every month whether to invest. That is usually how people fail. Life happens and there is always an emergency that requires cash. But future life happens too and you want to be spending your $50,000 a year, after inflation, not praying they won't cut Social Security benefits every year.

There is a clear reason why the working millionaires become wealthy. It is not luck or inheritance. Millions of immigrants to this country have done it before. They lived below their means. They invested in businesses they understood. They did not let temporary cash flow problems stop them from building wealth. They used the 10 steps of building wealth every day.

As many clients say, "I never even miss the contributions because I never see them. Then all of a sudden, I see my statement has $25,000, $50,000, $250,000, $500,000, $1,000,000. We are talking real money here."

That is *Your Hidden Gold Mine*.

You can start the dig TODAY. You will be surprised how easy it becomes over time. The $9 a day mining "expenses" are not too much to ask for your $250,000 or $1 million. Just put investing on automatic and wait to strike it rich!

Call Vanguard 800.551.8631 or TIAA-CREF 800.842.2888 today. Just do it! Thank me later.

Estimate of how long your portfolio will last

$5,833 per month
Spend 8% of your $500,000 each year
starting at age 65
$3,333 per month plus
Pension and Social Security 2,500 per month
90% chance of funds lasting to age 95
40% Stock, 60% Bond portfolio
(Inflation adjusted)

$4,166 per month
Spend 8% of your $250,000 each year
starting at age 65
$1,666 per month plus
Pension and Social Security 2,500 per month
90% chance of funds lasting to age 95
40% Stock, 60% Bond portfolio
(Inflation adjusted)

Estimates using 1,000 market return simulations at
https://www3.troweprice.com/ric/ricweb/public/ricResults.do
also:
http://www.bankrate.com/calculators/retirement/retirement-plan-income-calculator.aspx
http://cgi.money.cnn.com/tools/retirementplanner/retirementplanner.jsp

The Author

Law Steeple has been in financial services for over 20 years. He was a managing executive of the sales units of a number of bank securities firms. He is one of the insiders who contributed to the The Insiders Guides set of buyers' guides edited by Dan Keppel. The guides provide specific ways to save on all financial services. ***The Insiders' Guides to Buying Discount Financial Services: Buy Direct and Save $3,000 Every Year*** is available at Amazon, Barnes and Noble, Abebooks. Law lives in New Jersey and Florida.

To receive Dan Keppel's weekly Alert, go to www.TheInsidersGuides.com